THE BEST 50
OLIVE RECIPES

Catherine Pagano Fulde

BRISTOL PUBLISHING ENTERPRISES
San Leandro, California

Printed in the United States of America.

ISBN 1-55867-198-6

Cover design: Frank J. Paredes
Cover photography: John A. Benson
Food stylist: Susan Massey

THE INCOMPARABLE OLIVE

The olive is an extraordinary fruit, popular from the Mediterranean to the Americas. The Moroccans marry them with lemons; the Spanish, French, Italians and Greeks revere them. No dinner in Tunisia would be complete without them. Olives have made their way to Israel and Egypt. The Syrians, Lebanese and Jordanians enjoy them for breakfast. And here, in America, olive dishes are gracing the menus of the finest restaurants, replacing nuts and pretzels in the neighborhood bars and appearing in trios garnishing the "new" martini.

Why, then, is the olive so special? Since its cultivation in 3,000 BC, people have been enjoying this "gift of the gods." Throughout the centuries, the olive has been used for nourishment, healing, cleansing and even lubrication. It is believed that the Egyptians used its oil to move the blocks that built the pyramids!

What interests us today, however, is the culinary appeal and health benefits of olives. Olive oil's high ratio of monounsaturated fat to polyunsaturated fat means that it can actually lower cholesterol. A recent study published in *The Journal of the National Cancer Institute* discovered a connection between a high intake of olive oil and fiber to a low incidence of breast cancer. Despite the health advantages, a word of caution goes to dieters: 10 medium salt-cured olives coated with oil contain about 7 grams of fat.

Most people would consider an olive as a vegetable or garnish. In reality, the olive is the fleshy, bitter, pit-bearing, inedible fruit of the *oleacea olea europaea.* This fruit becomes edible only by *curing.* Curing is a method of preserving and flavoring foods. In the case of the olive, curing is necessary to remove the bitterness caused by a substance called oleuropein.

Curing methods have evolved from ancient times. Legend has it that a shipwrecked man discovered edible olive fruit on the beach. The salty sea water had leached the oleuropein from the olive flesh.

Today there are three main methods of curing olives: brine-curing, dry-curing and oil-curing.

- **Brine-curing** involves soaking green olives in an alkaline solution; then, fermenting the olives in brine or salt.

- **Dry-curing,** also called salt-curing, involves layering ripe olives with coarse salt and letting them stand until they are dry and wrinkled. The olives are then rubbed with oil.

- **Oil-curing** involves soaking ripe olives alternately in oil and water; then, the olives are rinsed under running water. This repetitive process takes several months.

It is a long journey from the tree to the table. Olive harvest begins in mid-autumn and continues through the winter. Over time, the bright green olives gain tinges of violet, then purple, then various shades of black. During this slow ripening process, some of the oleuropein changes to sugar. Olives are cured and seasoned throughout the stages of ripeness, lending a wide variety of flavors.

OLIVE VARIETIES

ALFONSO: Large, purple-black in color, meaty texture. Somewhat salty, but pleasant winey flavor. Brine-cured. From Chile.

CALIFORNIA RIPE BLACK: Sweet, buttery, very mild. Shiny black color. Available in all sizes, whole, pitted and sliced. Brine-cured.

CALIFORNIA RIPE GREEN: Similar to California ripe black, but green in color. Slight nutty flavor. Often stuffed with pimientos. Brine-cured.

CALIFORNIA SPANISH-STYLE: Full flavor, slightly salty. Green color. Available whole, pitted, stuffed and seasoned. Brine-cured.

FRENCH DATE: Medium to large in size and black in color. Smooth, creamy flesh. Salty, winey flavor. Vacuum-packed. Dry-cured.

GAETA: Available both brine-cured and dry-cured. Brine-cured Gaeta are small, plump and purple-black in color. Flesh is smooth, tender and flavorful. Dry-cured Gaeta are large and black with dry, wrinkled, oily flesh. Somewhat mild, yet flavorful. From Italy.

KALAMATA: Medium-sized, almond-shaped, purple-black in color. Smooth, firm flesh. Rich, intense flavor. Brine-cured. From Greece.

MANZANILLA: Green olive similar to California Spanish-style olive, but imported from Spain. Brine-cured.

MOROCCAN: Brine-cured and oil-cured. Moroccan olives are available. Brine-cured Moroccan olives are large, round and green with a salty, tart flavor. Available whole or cracked with spices. Dry-cured Moroccan olives are medium-sized, jet black in color, with oily, wrinkled flesh. Smoky, pleasantly bitter taste. Meaty and moist texture.

NIÇOISE: Small, brownish-green to black in color. Herbaceous, salty flavor. Brine-cured. From France.

PICHOLINE: Medium-sized, bullet-shaped, bright green in color. Sweet-salty flavor, crunchy texture. Brine-cured. From France.

SEVILLANO (QUEEN): Very large, round, medium-green in color. Mild taste and smooth texture. Brine-cured. From Spain.

SICILIAN: Available brine-cured and dry-cured. Brine-cured Sicilians are large, yellow-green, full-fleshed with intense flavor. Available whole, pitted, cracked or seasoned. Dry-cured Sicilians are similar to dry-cured Moroccans in appearance and texture. Flavorful, spicy and intense without bitter overtones.

TOSCANO: Large, oval, bright green in color. Crisp, smooth, flavorful. Similar to Picholine, but from Italy. Brine-cured.

FINDING OLIVES

The availability of olives in most U.S. cities is good, due to an increased interest in Mediterranean cooking. Many grocery stores now have olive bars for sampling prior to purchase. Supermarket gourmet sections feature bottles and jars of imported whole olives and olive products. Ethnic markets offer unadorned olives in vacuum-sealed pouches and seasoned olives from large vats.

STORING OLIVES

The shelf life of olives and olive products depends upon the packaging and the Ph factor. Opened jars of olives will keep up to 3 months under refrigeration, providing the brine is not contaminated by unsanitary utensils or hands. Always purchase bulk olives with their brine, or cover them with olive oil seasoned with spices and herbs; store them in the refrigerator and use them within 3 months. Save the oil when olives are gone for salads or cooking.

PITTING OLIVES

Several of the following recipes require that the olives are pitted; here are some tips:

- On a board, strike brine-cured olives with the back of a chef's knife or a meat mallet to crack the flesh. Remove the pit with a small knife or your fingers. For niçoise olives, use a sharp paring knife to cut the flesh from the pit.

- Grasp dry-cured or oil-cured olives between your thumb and first two fingers and squeeze out the pit. You can also use a small sharp knife.

- Some people believe cherry pitters or skewers to be effective tools for pitting olives, but these can be dangerous.

THE "NEW" MARTINI

*What would be the reaction of Guiseppi Martini,
the late 19th century inventor of the drink bearing his
name, if he could taste the current version of his libation?
It originally contained 1 part each dry and sweet
vermouth to 3 parts gin. Here is a basic recipe for the
"new" martini as served in the San Francisco Bay Area.*

dash (1/4 oz.) dry vermouth
8 shots (12 oz.) best-grade gin
crushed ice
6 small green olives, pitted and rinsed

Pour vermouth and gin over ice in a 1-quart pitcher. Stir briefly.
Strain mixture into 2 chilled martini glasses. Garnish each glass with
3 olives speared on a toothpick.

Servings: 2

MARINATED GREEN OLIVES

Brine-cured green olives combined with herbs
and spices make tasty, Mediterranean-style nibblers.
You can vary the flavor in infinite ways.

2 cups unseasoned green olives, drained and cracked
2 large cloves garlic, crushed
1/2 tsp. red pepper flakes
2 tsp. dried oregano, crushed
1/2 cup extra virgin olive oil

Combine all ingredients in a bowl and stir well. Transfer mixture to a covered jar and refrigerate for 3 days, mixing daily. Serve at room temperature. Keeps about 1 month in the refrigerator.

Makes about 2 1/2 cups

VARIATIONS

FRENCH-STYLE MARINATED OLIVES

Add ½ tsp. crushed fennel seeds, ½ tsp. crushed cumin seeds, ½ tsp. dried thyme and 1 large bay leaf. Reduce oregano to 1 tsp. Makes about 2½ cups.

SPANISH-STYLE MARINATED OLIVES

Add ⅓ cup golden raisins, 2 tbs. rinsed capers, 1 tbs. chopped fresh Italian parsley and 1 tbs. chopped fresh mint. Makes about 3 cups.

GREEK-STYLE MARINATED OLIVES

Add ½ cup red wine vinegar and the thinly sliced peel (zest) of 2 oranges and 1 lemon. Increase garlic to 4 cloves and olive oil to 1 cup. Makes about 3½ cups.

OLIVE-PISTACHIO PESTO

Toss these delicious sauces with hot cooked pasta. Or, be creative and combine your favorite olives with garlic, herbs and oil.

½ cup raw, unsalted, shelled pistachio nuts
1 shallot
1 cup pitted Toscano or California ripe green olives
¾ cup extra virgin olive oil
1 tbs. lemon juice
1 tbs. chopped fresh lemon peel (zest)
½ cup grated Parmesan cheese
salt and pepper to taste

With a food processor, process nuts and shallot to a smooth paste. Add olives and process until mixed. With machine running, add oil, lemon juice, lemon peel and cheese and process until smooth. Season with salt and pepper.

Makes: 1½ cups

VARIATION: GREEN OLIVE PESTO

With a food processor, process 1 cup pimiento-stuffed California ripe green olives, 3 cloves garlic, 1/4 cup chopped roasted red bell pepper, 1/4 cup chopped sun-dried tomatoes, 1/4 cup fresh basil leaves and 3 tbs. dry sherry until finely chopped. With machine running, slowly add 1/4 cup extra virgin olive oil and process until smooth. Makes 1 1/2 cups.

VARIATION: COOKED BLACK OLIVE PESTO

In a skillet, brown 3 cloves chopped garlic in 1/4 cup extra virgin olive oil. Add 1 cup chopped oil-cured black olives, 4 chopped anchovy fillets, 1 cup chicken, beef or vegetable stock, 1/4 cup fresh oregano leaves and pinch red pepper flakes; bring to a boil. Reduce heat to low and simmer covered for 5 minutes. Cool slightly and transfer to a food processor workbowl. Add 3 tbs. pine nuts and process until smooth. Makes 2 cups.

GREEN OLIVE TAPENADE

Try spooning this on ¼-inch-thick garden zucchini slices.

1 cup pitted Picholine olives
1 cup pitted California Spanish-
  style olives
2 tbs. capers, rinsed
2 anchovy fillets, drained
1 shallot, chopped

1 cup walnuts, toasted
1 tbs. California brandy
¼ cup extra virgin olive oil
3 tbs. walnut oil
2 tbs. snipped fresh basil
freshly ground pepper to taste

With a food processor, process olives, capers, anchovies, shallot and walnuts and brandy until coarsely chopped. With machine running, slowly add oils until mixture is blended, but still has some texture. Fold in basil and pepper and transfer to a serving bowl. Cover and refrigerate for 12 hours before serving.

Makes 2 cups

BLACK OLIVE TAPENADE

Serve this distinctively mellow tapenade on
grilled or toasted French bread rounds.

¾ cup pitted California ripe
    black olives
¾ cup pitted Kalamata olives
2 tbs. capers, rinsed
2 anchovy fillets, drained
2 cloves garlic, crushed
2 tbs. grated Parmesan cheese

¼ cup fresh Italian parsley
    leaves
2 tbs. sweet Marsala wine
¼ cup extra virgin olive oil
2 tbs. pine nuts, toasted
freshly ground pepper to taste

With a food processor, process olives, capers, anchovies, garlic, Parmesan, parsley and Marsala until coarsely chopped. With machine running, slowly add oil until mixture is blended, but still has some texture. Fold in nuts and pepper and transfer to a serving bowl. Cover and refrigerate for 12 hours before serving.

Makes 1½ cups

SWEET AND SOUR
EGGPLANT (CAPONATA)

*Caponata is to the Sicilians what fondue is to the Swiss —
the social dish! Serve it in a large ceramic bowl with a spoon
so friends can dollop it onto freshly sliced Italian bread.*

2 medium eggplants, peeled
   and cubed, about 8 cups
salt
1 cup extra virgin olive oil
2½ cups chopped celery
2 large onions, chopped
9 garlic cloves, minced
1 large red bell pepper,
   chopped, about 1½ cups
1 can (28 oz.) crushed
   tomatoes

1 can (6 oz.) artichoke hearts,
   rinsed and drained
1½ cups pitted California ripe
   black olives
1½ cups California Spanish-
   style olives with pimiento
1 cup capers, rinsed
½-¾ cup balsamic vinegar
2 tbs. sugar
salt and pepper to taste

Place eggplant in a colander, sprinkle with salt and drain for 1 hour.

In a large skillet, heat ½ cup of the olive oil over medium heat and sauté celery, onions, garlic and pepper until limp, about 15 minutes; set aside. Heat broiler. Rinse salt from eggplant and place on a foil-lined baking sheet moistened with extra-virgin olive oil; broil eggplant for about 12 minutes, turning halfway through cooking time, until soft. Add eggplant to skillet and heat gently over low heat. Add tomatoes, artichokes, olives and capers and simmer uncovered for 1 hour, stirring frequently. Add remaining olive oil, vinegar, sugar, salt and pepper; cool. Transfer mixture to a covered container and refrigerate for 3 days before serving, stirring daily to distribute liquid. Serve at room temperature. Keeps for up to 2 weeks.

Makes 3 quarts

RIPE OLIVE PRESERVE

*For an unusual, traditional Greek breakfast,
serve this exotic, easy-to-prepare condiment
with crusty peasant bread and feta cheese.*

1 cup pitted French date olives,
  rinsed
1¾ cups crushed fresh
  black figs

1 tbs. fresh lemon juice
2 tbs. sugar
¼ cup honey
¾ cup chopped fresh mint

In a 3-quart microwavable bowl, combine olives, figs, lemon juice, sugar and honey; mix well. Stir in 1 tbs. of the mint and microwave on HIGH for 10 minutes, stirring once. Stir in reserved mint and ladle into sterilized jars; cover tightly. Refrigerate when cool. Keeps for about 2 months.

Makes 1½ cups

MELON WITH BLACK OLIVES

Serve this summertime treat with drinks on the patio or as a colorful and tasty addition to the buffet table. Provide toothpicks for servers and a saucer for the olive pits and used toothpicks.

1 ripe orange-fleshed honeydew melon or cantaloupe
2 cups Gaeta or Kalamata olives
1 cup snipped fresh mint leaves

With a melon baller, scoop melon into balls. Or, cut melon into bite-sized cubes with a knife. Mix melon with olives and mint. Serve in a clear bowl.

Servings: 6

VARIATION: MELON, BLACK OLIVE AND WATERCRESS SALAD

Place mixture on a bed of watercress and dress with a mixture of olive oil, Meyer lemon juice, Midori liqueur, salt and pepper to taste.

Servings: 4

TOSCANO OLIVE BREAD

Make this bread in the bread machine or use the food processor for best results. To make with a bread machine, follow manufacturer's instructions and bake on the white or basic bread cycle. Make sure your bread machine can accommodate the amount of flour called for. Crushed olives provide moisture as well as flavor. Look for wheat gluten in health food stores.

3½ tsp. active dry yeast
¾ cup warm water
¼ cup extra virgin olive oil
1½ tsp. salt
1½ tsp. sugar
3½ cups unbleached all-purpose flour
2 tsp. wheat gluten
1 cup chopped Toscano olives

In a large liquid measuring cup, stir yeast into 1/4 cup of the water. Add oil, salt, sugar and remaining water to yeast mixture. Place flour and gluten in a food processor workbowl and pulse 3 times to mix. With machine running, slowly pour in yeast mixture. Add olives and process until dough forms a ball. Pulse 15 times to knead. Transfer dough to an oiled bowl. Cover with plastic wrap and let rise for 1½ to 2 hours until doubled in size. Transfer dough to a floured surface. Cut dough in half and shape into 1 or 2 thin ovals. Place ovals on an oiled baking sheet, cover with plastic wrap and let rise for 1 hour.

Heat oven to 400°. Bake bread for 35 to 40 minutes, until loaf sounds hollow when thumped. Cool on racks.

Makes 1 large or 2 medium loaves

FOCACCIA WITH BLACK OLIVES

*Focaccia makes a delicious afternoon snack. It is a healthful
alternative to chocolate chip cookies for after-school munching.
To make the dough with a bread machine, place ingredients in
the bread machine pan, reserving ½ of the oregano, thyme and
olives, and follow manufacturer's instructions for making dough.*

2 tsp. active dry yeast
¾ cup warm water
⅓ cup extra virgin olive oil, plus more for brushing
⅓ cup dry white wine
3½ cups unbleached all-purpose flour, or more if needed
½ tsp. sugar
½ tsp. salt
2 cups coarsely chopped Kalamata olives
2 tbs. chopped fresh oregano, or 1 tsp. dried
2 tbs. chopped fresh thyme, or 1 tsp. dried
sea salt for topping

In a large bowl, stir yeast into ¼ cup of the water and let stand for about 10 minutes, until creamy. Stir in remaining water, oil and wine. Add flour, sugar, salt, ½ of the olives, ½ of the oregano and ½ of the thyme. Mix well. Knead on a floured surface until smooth and velvety, adding additional flour if necessary. Place dough in a lightly oiled bowl, cover with plastic wrap and let rise until doubled in size, about 1½ hours.

Heat oven to 500°. Knead risen dough lightly on a floured surface. Pat or roll dough into a ¾-inch-thick rectangle and transfer to an oiled baking sheet. Sprinkle dough with sea salt and reserved thyme and oregano leaves. With your fingers, make several depressions in the surface of dough and press remaining olives into depressions. Bake on top oven rack for 25 minutes, until lightly browned. Brush with olive oil and cut into serving pieces.

Makes one 12-inch focaccia

PIZZA CATANIA-STYLE

This family recipe has a "no-cook" topping. Oil-cured black olives and sun-dried tomatoes provide the intense flavor. To make the dough with a bread machine, follow manufacturer's instructions for making dough. Thinly rolled French bread dough, available by the pound at most bread shops, works quite well in a pinch.

1½ tsp. active dry yeast
1 cup water
1 cup cake flour
2-2½ cups all-purpose flour
1 tsp. salt
1 jar (10 oz.) oil-packed sun-dried tomatoes, drained, oil reserved
2 cups halved oil-cured black olives
¼ cup chopped fresh oregano

¼ cup snipped fresh basil leaves
2 tins (2 oz. each) anchovy fillets, drained
4 large cloves garlic, very thinly sliced
¼ lb. provolone cheese, sliced and quartered, optional
sea salt to taste
red pepper flakes to taste
extra virgin olive oil for brushing

Dissolve yeast in ¼ cup of the warm water. In a large bowl, mix flours and salt. Make a well in the center of flour mixture and gradually pour in yeast mixture and remaining water, stirring until well mixed. Transfer dough to a floured surface and knead until smooth, about 10 minutes. Dough should still be quite wet. Place dough in an oiled bowl. Cover with plastic wrap and let rise for 2½ hours.

Heat oven to 500°. Cut dough into 2 equal pieces. Roll or stretch each piece into a 15-inch round and transfer each round to an oiled pizza pan. Brush dough with sun-dried tomato oil. Arrange remaining ingredients, except oil, decoratively on dough. Bake on bottom oven rack for 10 minutes, until crust is brown and topping is bubbly. Brush with olive oil and cut into wedges.

Makes two 15-inch pizzas

FRENCH PIZZA (PISSALADIÈRE)

For a taste of Provence, serve this classic country pizza with a simple tomato and herb salad and light, fruity wine. To make the dough with a bread machine, follow manufacturer's instructions.

2 tsp. active dry yeast
1 cup warm water
4½ cups all-purpose flour
1½ tsp. salt
3 medium-sized yellow onions, thinly sliced
¼ cup extra virgin olive oil
leaves from 3 sprigs fresh rosemary, about ¾ cup
salt and freshly ground pepper to taste
2-4 tsp. extra virgin olive oil, plus more for brushing
1 tin (2 oz.) anchovy fillets
⅔ cup halved Niçoise olives

Dissolve yeast in ¼ cup of the water. In a large bowl, mix flour with salt. Make a well in the center of flour mixture and gradually pour in yeast mixture and remaining water, stirring until well mixed. Transfer dough to a floured surface and knead until smooth, about 10 minutes. Dough should be quite firm. Place in an oiled bowl, cover with plastic wrap and let rise for 2½ hours.

Place onions, ¼ cup oil, rosemary, salt and pepper in a covered skillet and cook over medium-low heat until very soft and creamy, about 45 minutes, stirring occasionally.

Roll or stretch each dough piece into a 15-inch round and transfer each round to an oiled pizza pan. Cover dough and let rise for 30 minutes. Heat oven to 400°. Carefully brush dough with 2 to 4 tsp. oil and spread onion mixture evenly over the top. Arrange anchovies and olives on top of onion mixture. Season with pepper. Bake for 15 to 20 minutes, until crust is brown.

Makes two 15-inch pizzas

NEW ORLEANS SANDWICH (MUFFULETTA)

Reminiscent of the Philadelphia "Hoagie," the New England "Grinder" and the West Coast "Hero," the Muffuletta is the ultimate layered sandwich.

1 loaf (2 lb.) French or Italian bread, halved lengthwise
Olive Relish, follows
1/3 lb. Mortadella, thinly sliced
1/3 lb. dry salami, thinly sliced
1/3 lb. boiled ham, thinly sliced
1/4 lb. provolone cheese, thinly sliced
1/4 lb. mozzarella cheese, thinly sliced

Saturate both halves of bread with marinade from *Olive Relish*. Spread 1/2 of the olive relish on bottom bread half. Layer meats and cheeses over relish and spread remaining relish on top. Cover with remaining bread. Slice into serving pieces.

Servings: 5-6

OLIVE RELISH

1 cup chopped pimiento-
   stuffed California ripe
   green olives
1 cup chopped California
   ripe black olives
3/4 cup chopped roasted red
   or green bell peppers

2 cloves garlic, minced
2 tbs. chopped fresh Italian
   parsley
1 cup extra virgin olive oil
2 tsp. lemon juice
salt and pepper to taste

In a bowl, mix all ingredients; cover and refrigerate overnight to blend flavors.

Makes about 3 cups

GREEK PIZZA

Phyllo provides the crust and traditional Greek ingredients form the topping for this pizza. Kasseri is a sharp sheep's milk cheese.

8-10 sheets phyllo dough
1/4 cup extra virgin olive oil
1 green bell pepper, cut into
    1/4-inch-thick rounds
1 red bell pepper, cut into
    1/4-inch-thick rounds

3 cloves garlic, slivered
1 cup pitted Kalamata olives
2 tsp. capers, rinsed
1/2 lb. kasseri cheese, grated
dried Greek oregano to taste
red pepper flakes to taste

Heat oven to 400°. Layer phyllo sheets on an oiled baking sheet, brushing each sheet with oil. Arrange peppers, garlic, olives and capers on top of dough and sprinkle with cheese, oregano and pepper flakes. Drizzle remaining oil over the top. Bake for 30 minutes. Let stand for 5 minutes before serving.

Servings: 6-8

ORANGE, OLIVE AND FENNEL SALAD

The citrus flavor of this salad is refreshing after a heavy meal.

1 clove garlic, halved
⅓ cup extra virgin olive oil
⅓ cup orange juice
salt and freshly ground
   pepper to taste
leaves from 2 bunches arugula

4 navel oranges, peel and pith
   removed, sliced crosswise
1 large bulb fennel, halved
   and thinly sliced
½ cup pitted oil-cured black
   olives

Rub a large salad bowl several times with cut surface of garlic clove; discard garlic. In bowl, whisk olive oil, orange juice, salt and pepper. Add arugula to bowl and toss with dressing; transfer salad to chilled serving dishes. Add oranges, fennel and olives to bowl with dressing; mix well and arrange over arugula on plates. Sprinkle with additional salt and pepper.

Servings: 4

TOMATO, BLACK OLIVE AND FETA SALAD

Since tomatoes are a major component of this salad, it is especially important to use the finest quality you can find. French feta is less salty than other varieties.

2 tbs. balsamic vinegar
¼ cup extra virgin olive oil
salt and freshly ground pepper
   to taste
8-10 large Roma tomatoes
1 cup pitted Kalamata olives

1 cup thinly sliced red onion
5 cups prepared bitter salad
   greens, such as arugula,
   chicory and endive
1 cup crumbled French feta
   cheese

Whisk vinegar with olive oil in a large bowl and season with salt and pepper. Add tomatoes, olives, onion and greens to bowl and toss well. Top with feta cheese and additional ground pepper.

Servings: 4

COUSCOUS, GARBANZO AND OLIVE SALAD

Serve this multi-ethnic salad as an inspired one-dish dinner.

1/4 cup lemon juice
3/4 cup extra virgin olive oil
salt and pepper to taste
2 1/2 cups boiling water
2 cups instant couscous
2 cans (15 1/2 oz. each) garbanzo
  beans, rinsed and drained
3 tbs. capers, rinsed

1 jar (7 oz.) roasted red bell
  peppers, drained, chopped
1 cup pitted Gaeta olives,
  plus more for garnish
2 cloves garlic, minced
1/4 cup chopped green onions
1/3 cup chopped fresh mint
tomato wedges for garnish

In a small bowl, whisk lemon juice with oil, salt and pepper. In a large bowl, pour water over couscous, cover and let stand for about 10 minutes, until water is absorbed; fluff grains with a fork. Fold remaining ingredients, except garnishes, into couscous and add dressing. Mix well and chill. Serve salad garnished with tomatoes and olives.

Servings: 6-8

OLIVE PASTA SALAD WITH FAVA BEANS AND FENNEL

Fava beans are similar to lima beans. They and sweet fennel combine well with salty green olives and pasta.

1½ cups shelled fava beans (½ to ¾ lb. unshelled)
1 large yellow onion, thinly sliced
1 cup thinly sliced fennel bulb, with some of the feathery leaves
¼ cup extra virgin olive oil
12 large green Sicilian olives, coarsely chopped
1 tbs. chopped fresh orange peel (zest)
½ tsp. red pepper flakes
salt to taste
2 cups orchiette pasta
shaved Parmesan cheese

Cook fava beans for 10 seconds in a large pot of boiling salted water. With a slotted spoon, transfer beans to a bowl of ice water; drain. Remove and discard tough outer skin from fava beans; set aside. Steam onion and fennel until soft, about 20 minutes. In a large bowl, combine fava beans with onion, fennel, olive oil, olives, orange peel and red pepper flakes. Cook orchiette in a large pot of boiling salted water until slightly firm to the bite, *al dente*. Drain pasta and mix well with vegetable mixture, taking care not to crush beans. Top with shaved Parmesan cheese. Serve warm.

Servings: 4

WILTED SPINACH WITH OLIVE-COATED GOAT CHEESE

*Baked goat cheese coated with olive breadcrumbs provides
a creamy accent to the slightly salty spinach salad.*

4 slices bacon, cut into 1-inch slices
1 tbs. extra virgin olive oil
2 tsp. balsamic vinegar
1/4 tsp. garlic powder
2 small bunches spinach, washed, stems removed, spun dry
12 Kalamata olives, sliced
salt and pepper to taste
3 Kalamata olives, finely chopped
1 1/2 cups fresh breadcrumbs
1 log (8 oz.) goat cheese, cut into 8 slices
2 cups unseasoned croutons

In a large skillet, sauté bacon over medium-high heat until crisp and brown. With a slotted spoon, transfer bacon to a paper towel and pour all but 2 tbs. drippings from skillet. Whisk olive oil, vinegar and garlic powder into skillet with bacon drippings and heat through. Add spinach and sliced olives to skillet and season with salt and pepper; stir well and set aside.

Heat oven to 400°. In a shallow dish, mix finely chopped olives with fresh breadcrumbs. Carefully coat cheese slices with olive-breadcrumb mixture and place on an oiled baking sheet. Bake for 5 to 6 minutes, until lightly browned. Serve salad on serving plates topped with bacon and croutons. Place baked cheese slices on the side.

Servings: 4

BREAD SALAD (PANZANELLA)

In this dish, stale, crusty Italian bread is transformed into a heavenly salad with the addition of fruity extra virgin olive oil, fresh basil and a few vegetables. Said to be of Tuscan origin, this version of panzanella has Sicilian roots.

2 red onions
8 thick slices stale Italian bread, oven-toasted
2 tbs. red wine vinegar or balsamic vinegar
½ cup fruity extra virgin olive oil
salt and pepper to taste
8 garden tomatoes, cut into eighths
2 cucumbers, peeled and thinly sliced
1 small bunch radishes, thinly sliced
2 stalks celery, thinly sliced
1 cup chopped cracked Sicilian green olives

3 tsp. capers, rinsed
4 anchovy fillets, chopped
1/4 cup chopped fresh basil

Thinly slice onions and soak in cold water for 1 hour; drain.
Soak bread in cold water for 5 minutes until very moist. In a small bowl, whisk vinegar with oil, salt and pepper; set aside. Squeeze water from bread and shred bread into a large serving bowl with your fingers. Add remaining ingredients, including onions and dressing, and toss until well mixed. Serve at room temperature.

Servings: 8-10

SHELLFISH SALAD

Mussels, shrimp and clams combine with green and black olives, tomatoes, herbs, wine and extra virgin olive oil in a dish from the Adriatic Coast. Serve at room temperature with an icy-cold, dry white wine.

1 cup dry white wine
1 clove garlic, smashed
two 4-inch sprigs fresh thyme
2 lb. fresh mussels, beards removed and scrubbed
1½ lb. medium shrimp, scrubbed
2 lb. small fresh clams, scrubbed
8 brine-cured green olives
8 brine-cured black olives, halved, plus more for garnish

4 ripe tomatoes, cut into sixths
¼ cup fresh basil leaves, stacked, rolled and snipped into fine slivers
2 tbs. finely chopped fresh lemon peel (zest)
¼ cup extra virgin olive oil
1 tbs. lemon juice
green or red lettuce leaves
lemon wedges for garnish
basil sprigs for garnish

In a large skillet, bring wine, garlic and thyme to a boil. Reduce heat to low and keep at a simmer. Add shellfish to pan in batches and cook, covered, until mussel and clam shells open and shrimp turn pink, about 8 minutes for each batch. Do not overcook. Strain cooking liquid, reserving 1/4 cup. Reserve 8 mussels and 8 clams for garnish and remove remaining shellfish from shells. In a large bowl, combine shellfish, olives, tomatoes, snipped basil, lemon peel, olive oil and lemon juice. Add just enough of the reserved cooking liquid to moisten ingredients. Chill salad covered for at least 2 hours. Remove salad from refrigerator 20 minutes before serving. Serve on lettuce-lined plates and garnish with reserved clams, mussels, lemon wedges, basil sprigs and olives.

Servings: 4

MEXICAN BEAN SOUP

Warm buttered cornbread complements this spicy soup.
Sliced olives and sour cream tone down the soup's heat.

3 tbs. canola oil
3 chorizo sausages, casings
  removed
4 sprigs fresh Italian parsley
4 sprigs fresh thyme
4 sprigs fresh marjoram
4 sprigs fresh oregano
5 large cloves garlic, crushed
2 cups chopped onions
2 cups chopped celery
2 cups chopped carrots
2 cups chopped tomatoes

2 small jalapeño peppers,
  seeded and chopped
2 bay leaves, crumbled
3 tsp. ground cumin
3 tsp. chili powder
1 lb. dried pinto beans, soaked
  overnight and drained
1 cup chopped Sevillano olives
8-10 cups chicken stock
sliced olives for garnish
sour cream for garnish

In a large stockpot, heat canola oil over medium-high heat and quickly brown chorizos. Pour off excess fat. Tie herb sprigs together with kitchen string and add to pot with garlic, onions, celery, carrots, tomatoes, jalapeños, bay leaves, cumin and chili powder. Cook, stirring constantly, until vegetables are browned. Add beans, chopped olives and 8 cups stock and bring to a boil. Reduce heat to low and simmer covered for 2½ hours, adding additional stock if soup thickens too rapidly.

Remove herb bundle and bay leaf. Carefully process soup with a food processor, in batches if necessary, until smooth. Return soup to stockpot and heat through. Ladle into bowls and garnish with sliced olives and sour cream.

Servings: 4-6

POTATO, OLIVE AND CHEDDAR SOUP

*Ripe olives lend a buttery richness to this smooth,
flavorful soup. Try it with cheesy homemade croutons.*

3 tbs. butter
½ cup finely chopped onion
½ cup finely chopped celery
½ cup finely chopped fresh Italian parsley
3 cloves garlic, crushed
5 cups chicken stock
dash lemon juice
4 medium potatoes, peeled and chopped
salt and pepper to taste
½ cup heavy cream, optional
2 cups grated cheddar cheese
1 cup sliced California ripe black olives, drained on paper towels
sliced black olives for garnish
chopped fresh chives for garnish

In a heavy stockpot, melt butter over medium heat. Add onion, celery, parsley and garlic and sauté until soft. Add stock, lemon juice, potatoes, salt and pepper and bring to a boil. Reduce heat to low and simmer covered for 20 to 30 minutes, until potatoes are soft. Carefully process soup with a food processor, in batches if necessary, until smooth. Return mixture to stockpot and add cream, if using, cheese and olives. Simmer for 5 minutes, stirring constantly. Serve garnished with olives and chopped chives.

Servings: 6

OLIVE GAZPACHO

This summer treat boasts smooth olives and crunchy vegetables.
Garnish with additional fresh herbs, olives and cucumber slices.

1 red onion, chopped
1 green bell pepper, chopped
1 red bell pepper, chopped
2 large tomatoes, chopped
1 large cucumber, seeded and
   chopped
1 cup pimiento-stuffed
   California ripe green olives

$\frac{1}{4}$ cup chopped fresh cilantro
$\frac{1}{4}$ cup chopped fresh parsley
3 cups tomato juice
$\frac{1}{3}$ cup olive oil
$\frac{1}{4}$ cup red wine vinegar
$\frac{1}{4}$ tsp. hot pepper sauce
salt to taste

Mix all ingredients in a large bowl. Process mixture with a food processor, in batches if necessary, until blended, but still slightly chunky. Cover and chill for 6 hours before serving.

Servings: 4-6

OLIVES COOKED IN TOMATO SAUCE

Here, olives are treated as a vegetable to accompany grilled foods.

1½ lb. mixed brine-cured green and black olives, halved
4 cloves garlic, minced
⅓ cup extra virgin olive oil
2 cups chopped fresh tomatoes
2 tbs. tomato paste mixed with ½ cup water
two ¼-inch-thick slices lemon
two ¼-inch-thick slices orange
salt to taste
red pepper flakes to taste
¼ cup chopped fresh Italian parsley

Plunge olives into boiling water and bring to a second boil; drain. In a large skillet, brown garlic in oil and add tomatoes and tomato paste mixture. Cook over high heat for 3 minutes, stirring constantly. Reduce heat to low and add olives, lemon, orange, salt and pepper flakes; simmer for 5 minutes, until thickened. Pour into a serving bowl, remove fruit and top with parsley. Serve hot or cold.

Servings: 4

BROILED VEGETABLES WITH OLIVES

For a quick, healthful dinner, toss these veggies with penne pasta.

4 medium Japanese eggplants
4 small red potatoes
4 large Roma tomatoes
2 long zucchini
1 red bell pepper
1 green bell pepper
½ cup extra virgin olive oil

¼ cup chopped fresh basil
¼ cup chopped fresh oregano
salt and pepper to taste
½ cup cracked green
   Moroccan olives
½ cup Alfonso olives

Heat broiler. Cut eggplant and potatoes crosswise into ¼-inch slices. Cut tomatoes and zucchini into ½-inch slices. Cut peppers into 2-x-2-inch strips. Place vegetables on a foil-lined baking sheet and sprinkle with oil, herbs, salt and pepper. Add olives and mix well. Broil mixture 4 inches from heat source for about 5 minutes. Turn and cook until vegetables are slightly charred, about 8 minutes.

Servings: 4

BAKED POTATOES, SWEET ONIONS AND GREEN OLIVES

*Try this variation of scalloped potatoes
the next time you prepare an oven dinner.*

3 tbs. extra virgin olive oil
4 large baking potatoes, peeled
  and cut into 1/4-inch rounds
1 medium sweet onion, thinly
  sliced
1 tbs. capers, rinsed

1 cup sliced Sicilian green
  olives
1/2 cup chopped fresh Italian
  parsley
salt and white pepper to taste
2 eggs beaten with 1 cup milk

Heat oven to 350°. Coat a 9-x-11-inch baking dish with olive oil. In pan, layer potatoes, onion, capers, olives and parsley twice, sprinkling layers with salt and pepper. Pour egg-milk mixture over the top. Cover pan with aluminum foil and bake for 30 minutes. Remove foil and bake for 10 to 15 minutes, until top is golden.

Servings: 4

PEPPERS STUFFED WITH EGGPLANT AND OLIVES

Stuffing vegetables with other vegetables and savory items dates back to the Renaissance courts. For ease, purchase tomato paste in a tube. Choose peppers with a flattened bottom, so that they will stand upright in a baking pan after being stuffed.

6 yellow bell peppers
½ cup extra virgin olive oil
6 Japanese eggplants, cut into small cubes
¼ cup tomato paste
½ cup water
¾ cup chopped Gaeta olives
1 tbs. capers, rinsed and chopped
¾ cup chopped toasted almonds
salt and freshly ground pepper to taste

Heat broiler. Place peppers on a foil-lined baking sheet and broil about 4 inches from heat source until skin darkens and blisters, turning to char all sides. Place charred peppers in a sealed paper bag and let stand until cool. Remove skin, stems, ribs and seeds, leaving peppers whole, and set peppers aside.

Reduce oven heat to 375°. Heat ½ of the oil in a skillet over medium-high heat. Sauté eggplant cubes a few at a time until cooked through and lightly browned. Mix tomato paste with water and pour over eggplant. Add olives, capers, almonds, salt and pepper to skillet and mix well. Fill pepper cavities with eggplant mixture and arrange peppers upright in a deep baking dish. Drizzle stuffed peppers with remaining olive oil and bake for 30 minutes, until heated through. Cool and serve at room temperature.

Servings: 6

ZUCCHINI, TOMATO AND OLIVE GRATIN

Garden-fresh produce makes the difference in this delightful dish. Serve it with all grilled foods. Fontina cheese is a semifirm cow's milk cheese with a mild, nutty flavor.

½ cup sliced California ripe black olives
2 medium onions, thinly sliced
3 cloves garlic, minced
1 tbs. fresh thyme
2 tbs. fresh oregano
¼ cup extra virgin olive oil
four 2-inch-diameter zucchini, cut into ¼-inch-thick slices
6 medium Roma tomatoes, cut into ¼-inch-thick slices
1 cup fresh basil leaves

10 large Alfonso olives, halved
salt and freshly ground pepper to taste
½ cup grated fontina cheese, optional
¼ cup pine nuts, toasted, optional
½ cup coarse dry breadcrumbs, toasted, optional
¼ cup extra virgin olive oil, optional

Heat oven to 350°. In a skillet, sauté sliced olives, onions, garlic, 1 tsp. of the thyme, 2 tsp. of the oregano and 3 tbs. of the olive oil over medium heat until soft, but not brown. Spread mixture in a shallow 9-x-11-inch baking pan. Arrange zucchini and tomato slices in alternating rows on top of onion mixture, placing basil leaves and halved olives in between vegetable slices. Sprinkle with remaining herbs, drizzle with remaining olive oil and season with salt and pepper. Bake for about 30 minutes, until vegetables are tender.

If desired, mix cheese, nuts and breadcrumbs in a bowl. Sprinkle breadcrumb mixture over baked vegetables and drizzle with 1/4 cup olive oil. Bake for additional 5 minutes, until golden brown.

Servings: 4-6

SWISS CHARD, BEANS AND OLIVES

Freshness is paramount with this summertime treat. Cranberry beans are fresh shelling beans that are streaked with red.

1 lb. fresh cranberry beans, shelled (about 1 cup)
1 small red onion, thinly sliced
1/4 cup extra virgin olive oil
1 bunch young Swiss chard, leaves cut into 2-inch ribbons (about 6-8 cups)

3/4 cup pitted California ripe black olives
salt and pepper to taste
2 oz. Stilton or other flavorful blue cheese, crumbled

Boil beans in water for 15 minutes, until tender-crisp; drain. In a large skillet, sauté onion in oil over medium heat until wilted. Add beans and cook for 3 minutes. Add chard and cook, stirring, for 3 to 5 minutes, until wilted and tender-crisp. Stir in olives. Season with salt and pepper and top with crumbled cheese.

Servings: 4

EXOTIC RICE WITH BABY SHRIMP

*Reminiscent of paella, this dish is quickly
prepared and can be doubled or tripled for a crowd.*

½ medium onion, thinly sliced
¼ cup peanut oil
1 cup jasmine rice
½ cup diced ripe tomato
½ cup diced roasted red bell
 pepper
¼ cup quartered oil-cured olives

½ cup quartered green olives
1 can (14½ oz.) chicken broth
2 pinches saffron threads
¼ cup clam juice
pinch hot pepper flakes
½ tsp. ground cumin
½ lb. cooked baby shrimp

In a large skillet, sauté onion in oil over medium heat until soft.
Add rice and stir constantly until opaque. Add remaining ingredients
and mix well. Reduce heat to low, cover and simmer for 20 minutes,
until liquid is absorbed and rice is fluffy.

Servings: 4-6

"LADIES OF THE NIGHT" PASTA (PASTA PUTTANESCA)

In Italy, one legend tells that prostitutes lured customers into their establishments with the seductive aroma of this easily prepared dish. Another states that unfaithful wives returning from their trysts hastily prepared this dish for dinner. Either way, it is a zesty palate-pleaser.

1 lb. spaghetti
6 tbs. extra virgin olive oil
2 cloves garlic, minced
3 anchovy fillets, drained and mashed
1 can (28 oz.) chopped tomatoes, drained
1 tbs. capers, rinsed and chopped
¾ cup coarsely chopped oil-cured Sicilian olives
¼ tsp. red pepper flakes
toasted breadcrumbs or grated Pecorino Romano cheese

Cook spaghetti in a large amount of boiling salted water until slightly firm to the bite, *al dente*; drain and keep warm. In a skillet, heat oil over medium heat and sauté garlic until aromatic. Add anchovies and stir until dissolved. Add tomatoes, capers, olives and red pepper flakes to skillet. Increase heat to high and cook mixture for 10 to 15 minutes, stirring often, until oil separates. In a warm bowl, combine pasta with sauce and toss to mix well. Serve pasta topped with breadcrumbs or cheese.

Servings: 4-6

RADIATORE WITH TOMATO-OLIVE SAUCE

Carrots, onions and celery are the "holy trinity" of Italian cooking. Combining them with tomatoes, garlic and green and black olives lends magic results. Substitute any ridged pasta for the radiatore. Ricotta salata is a salted, aged version of ricotta cheese. In this form, it is a hard, dry grating cheese with a sharp flavor.

1 lb. radiatore
¼ cup extra virgin olive oil
½ cup finely chopped carrots
½ cup finely chopped celery
2 cups finely chopped onions
3 cloves garlic, minced
4 cups chopped fresh tomatoes
¼ tsp. sugar
¼ tsp. salt

¼ tsp. freshly ground pepper
½ cup chopped green olives
½ cup chopped brine-cured black olives
1 tbs. chopped fresh basil
1 tbs. chopped fresh oregano
grated ricotta salata or Pecorino Romano cheese

Cook radiatore in a large amount of boiling salted water until slightly firm to the bite, *al dente*; drain and keep warm. In a large skillet, heat oil over medium-high heat and sauté carrots, celery, onions and garlic until golden brown. Add tomatoes, sugar, salt and pepper to skillet and cook over high heat for 10 to 15 minutes, stirring often, until thick and creamy. Reduce heat to low and add olives and herbs, stirring until blended. In a serving bowl, mix sauce with pasta and serve topped with cheese.

Servings: 4-6

ANGEL HAIR PASTA WITH SEA BASS AND OLIVES

Fresh mint gives this quick sauté its refreshing character.
Squeeze lemon juice over the pasta to brighten the flavors.

12 oz. angel hair pasta (capellini)
¼ cup plus 2 tbs. extra virgin olive oil
4 cloves garlic, thinly sliced
1 lb. Chilean sea bass fillets, cut into 1½-inch squares
1½ cups Roma tomato wedges
¾ cup pitted Kalamata olives
3 tbs. capers, rinsed
¼ cup chopped fresh oregano
¼ cup chopped fresh basil
2 tbs. chopped fresh mint
salt and freshly ground pepper to taste
lemon wedges

Cook angel hair pasta in a large amount of boiling salted water until slightly firm to the bite, *al dente*; drain and keep warm. In a heavy-bottomed skillet, heat 1/4 cup oil over medium-high heat and sauté garlic cloves until lightly browned; discard garlic. Add sea bass to skillet and sauté until browned, about 8 minutes. Add tomatoes, olives, capers, oregano, basil, mint, salt and pepper to skillet and sauté quickly until juice is released from tomatoes and ingredients are heated through, about 3 to 4 minutes. Add drained pasta and remaining olive oil to skillet and mix well. Serve immediately with lemon wedges to squeeze over individual servings.

Servings: 4

RIGATONI WITH EGGPLANT

Chewy rigatoni sets off the oh-so-Mediterranean combination of roasted vegetables, olives, anchovies and capers in this rustic presentation. Use the freshest possible vegetables you can find.

½ lb. rigatoni
1½ lb. eggplant, cut into 1½-inch cubes
1 red bell pepper, cut into 1½-inch pieces
1 green bell pepper, cut into 1½-inch pieces
2 large cloves garlic, thinly sliced
1 cup sliced Kalamata olives
4 anchovy fillets, drained and snipped into thirds
2 tbs. capers, rinsed
¼ cup extra virgin olive oil, or more if needed
¼ cup chopped fresh oregano
salt and freshly ground pepper to taste
grated Pecorino Romano cheese to taste

Cook rigatoni in a large amount of boiling salted water until slightly firm to the bite, *al dente*; drain and keep warm. Heat broiler. Combine eggplant, peppers, garlic, olives, anchovies and capers in a shallow roasting pan. Add oil, oregano, salt and pepper and mix until vegetables are well coated with oil. Broil vegetables 4 inches from heat source for about 10 minutes. Stir and broil for 5 additional minutes, or until vegetables are cooked through. In a large serving bowl, mix vegetables with rigatoni and grated cheese. Add a small amount of olive oil if mixture seems too dry. Serve immediately.

Servings: 4

ORANGE RICE

Pitted green olives add a salty tang to this fragrant dish. This dish can also be made with a rice cooker, but reduce the amount of orange juice to 1 cup.

1 cup water
1½ cups orange juice
1 cup basmati rice
½ cup chopped Manzanilla olives
1 tbs. grated fresh orange peel (zest)
salt and white pepper to taste

In a saucepan, bring water and orange juice to a boil. Stir in rice and return to boil. Reduce heat to very low, cover and cook until liquid evaporates and rice is tender, about 15 to 18 minutes. Transfer rice to a warm bowl and stir in olives, orange peel, salt and pepper. Cover and let stand for 5 minutes to blend flavors.

Servings: 4

LEMON-GRILLED SALMON WITH OLIVES

*A simple marriage of flavors enhances delicate salmon.
Garnish with lemon wedges, parsley sprigs and pitted
olives and serve on a bed of fresh spinach leaves.*

4 fresh salmon steaks, about
  6 oz. each
salt
lemon pepper seasoning
juice of 2 lemons mixed with
  1/3 cup canola oil

1 cup sour cream
3/4 cup chopped California
  ripe black olives
3 tsp. chopped fresh chives
1 tsp. chopped fresh lemon
  peel (zest)

Heat grill to medium-high. Season salmon liberally with salt and lemon pepper, brush with juice mixture and let stand for 10 minutes. Mix remaining ingredients to make a sauce. Brush salmon again with juice mixture. Grill salmon for 2½ to 3 minutes per side, basting frequently, until fish flakes easily. Pass sauce.

Servings: 4

"SALT COD" WITH OLIVES

An olive cookbook would not be complete without Baccalà, a traditional preparation for salted cod. Unfortunately, the authentic, time-intensive preparation is too much for most of us. Here, the method has been modified without much loss of flavor.

2 lb. Alaskan cod fillets, about
    1½-inch-thick, cut into
    2-inch squares
salt
about ½ cup extra virgin
    olive oil
2 onions, chopped
4 cloves garlic, crushed
1 cup chopped celery
1 lb. potatoes, peeled and
    cut into ½-inch-thick slices

1 can (28 oz.) crushed
    tomatoes
1½ cups water
1 tsp. dried oregano
1 bay leaf
1 cup pitted green olives
2 tbs. capers, rinsed
salt and coarsely ground
    pepper to taste
1 cup chopped fresh Italian
    parsley

Sprinkle cod pieces liberally with salt and let stand for 5 minutes; wipe dry. In a large skillet, heat ½ of the oil over medium-high heat and brown salted cod on both sides; remove cod and set aside. Add onions, garlic and celery to skillet and sauté over medium heat until soft, adding more oil as needed. Add potatoes, cover skillet and cook for 40 minutes, stirring occasionally. Remove skillet from heat and add remaining ingredients, except cod and parsley. Mix gently. Cover and simmer for 20 minutes. Stir in cod and cook for about 5 minutes, until cod is heated through and sauce is thick. Stir in parsley. Serve immediately.

Servings: 6

SWORDFISH ALLA GHIOTTA

The sweet-sour flavors of Sicily come together in this simple dish.

6 swordfish steaks, about
  ½-inch thick
¼ cup extra virgin olive oil, or
  more if needed
1 large onion, thinly sliced
2 stalks celery, thinly sliced
2 cups tomato sauce

½ cup capers, rinsed
2 cups mixed chopped green
  and black Sicilian olives
¼ cup raisins
salt and pepper to taste
3 tbs. pine nuts, toasted, for
  garnish

In a skillet, quickly brown swordfish in oil over medium-high heat on both sides; set aside. Add onion and celery to skillet and sauté until soft, adding more oil if needed. Add tomato sauce, capers and olives, reduce heat to low and simmer covered for 10 minutes. Return fish to skillet, spooning sauce over fish. Add raisins, salt and pepper and simmer covered for 5 minutes. Serve garnished with nuts.

Servings: 6

CHICKEN PROVENÇAL

This combination of flavors brings France to your table.

3½-4 lb. chicken pieces
flour seasoned with salt and
 pepper
¼ cup extra virgin olive oil
2 shallots, chopped
1 clove garlic, chopped
1 tbs. herbes de Provence

1 can (28 oz.) chopped
 tomatoes, drained
3 tbs. anise-flavored liqueur,
 such as pastis or Pernod
1 cup dry white wine
¾ cup pitted Niçoise olives

Heat oven to 350°. Dredge chicken in seasoned flour. In a skillet, brown chicken in oil a few pieces at a time and transfer chicken to a shallow roasting pan. Lightly brown shallots and garlic in skillet and add herbs, tomatoes, liqueur and wine. Cook over high heat for 5 minutes, stirring often. Mix in olives and pour over chicken. Bake chicken for 20 minutes, or until sauce is thick and bubbling.

Servings: 6

HUNTER'S-STYLE BRAISED PORK

Slow simmering tenderizes pork and brings out its mellow flavor. Olives add character and tartness to the dish, while rosemary and juniper berries add complexity.

1½ lb. boneless pork steak, cut into 1½-inch cubes
1 onion, coarsely chopped
2 cloves garlic, coarsely chopped
three 4-inch sprigs fresh rosemary
1 tsp. juniper berries
2 cups dry red wine, or more if needed
flour for dredging
½ cup extra virgin olive oil
salt and pepper to taste

garlic powder to taste
1 cup ¼-inch-thick onion slices
2 cups ½-inch-thick diagonal carrot slices
1 cup quartered small Roma tomatoes
1 cup pitted green olives
¼ cup gin
1 large sprig fresh rosemary
4 juniper berries
3 cups beef stock
1 cup frozen peas, thawed

Combine pork, chopped onion, garlic, 3 rosemary sprigs, 1 tsp. juniper berries and 1 cup of the red wine in a locking plastic bag. Seal tightly and refrigerate overnight, but not more than 24 hours.

Heat oven to 325°. Lift meat from marinade, wipe dry and dredge in flour. Heat 1/4 cup of the oil in a large skillet over medium-high heat. Brown pork cubes well on all sides, seasoning with salt, pepper and garlic powder; remove and set aside. Toss sliced onions, carrots, tomatoes and olives separately in flour and brown each item separately in skillet, adding oil as needed; set aside. Mix gin with 1 cup of the wine and pour into skillet, scraping up the browned bits. Transfer all browned items, including pan drippings, to a deep, 2-quart ovenproof pan. Add large sprig rosemary, 4 juniper berries and beef stock and mix well. If necessary, add wine so that liquid is 2 inches higher than meat and vegetables. Cover pan tightly and bake until pork is very tender, about 1 to 1 1/2 hours. Stir in peas during the last 10 minutes of cooking.

Servings: 4

BEEF-OLIVE ROULADE

This elegant stuffed beef roll can be served hot or cold. To make olive paste, puree pitted olives with a food processor. Demi-glace, a beef-flavored concentrate, is available at gourmet stores.

1½ lb. top sirloin steak, cut
   into ½-inch thick slices
1½ cups fresh Italian parsley
   leaves
5 cloves garlic, minced
1 cup fresh breadcrumbs
3 large red bell peppers,
   roasted, peeled, seeded
   and cut into thirds

1 cup Kalamata olive paste
¼ cup extra virgin olive oil
few grinds black pepper
1 cup dry red wine or beef stock
1 tsp. demi-glace, dissolved
   in 3 tsp. water
chopped fresh parsley for garnish
Kalamata olives for garnish

With a mallet, pound steak until ¼-inch thick. With a food processor, process parsley and garlic until finely minced. Add breadcrumbs and pulse 12 times until well blended.

Heat broiler. Lay pounded steak flat on a work surface and cover steak with pepper slices, peeled side down, leaving a 1-inch border. Spread olive paste over peppers and sprinkle with breadcrumb mixture. Drizzle 3 tbs. of the olive oil over breadcrumbs and sprinkle with pepper. Roll steak jelly roll-fashion, folding free border in over stuffing. Secure with skewers. Brush tops of rolls with remaining olive oil and place rolls seam-side down on an oiled rack in a shallow roasting pan. Broil beef rolls 4 inches from heat source for 18 to 20 minutes for medium-rare, or 23 to 25 minutes for medium-well, turning halfway through cooking time. Carefully transfer beef rolls to a cutting board and let stand for 5 minutes. Add 1 cup wine to roasting pan and stir in demi-glace mixture. Heat on the stovetop over medium-high heat, scraping up the browned bits. Cut rolls into $\frac{1}{2}$-inch-thick slices and place on a serving platter. Garnish with parsley and whole olives. Pass drippings separately.

Servings: 4

BRAISED LAMB WITH OLIVES AND DATES

Moroccan dry-cured black olives are showcased in this traditional stew. The contrast of spicy, salty and sweet flavors enhances the succulent braised lamb.

¼ cup extra virgin olive oil
3 lb. boneless lamb leg or shoulder, trimmed and cut into 2-inch cubes
2 cloves garlic, minced
1 large onion, thinly sliced
1 tsp. grated fresh ginger
1 tsp. cinnamon
1 tsp. ground allspice
¼ tsp. cayenne pepper
¼ tsp. powdered saffron
about 1 cup dry red wine
1 cup water

salt and pepper to taste
¾ cup halved dry-cured Moroccan olives, plus more for garnish
1 cup chopped dates, plus more for garnish
½ cup chopped fresh Italian parsley
½ cup chopped fresh cilantro, plus more for garnish
2 tsp. honey
3 tbs. sesame seeds, toasted

In a large skillet, heat 3 tbs. of the oil over medium-high heat. Sauté lamb in small batches until browned on all sides; remove lamb from skillet and set aside. In remaining oil, sauté garlic and onion until very soft. Return browned lamb to pan with ginger, cinnamon, allspice, cayenne, saffron, 1 cup wine, water, salt and pepper. Cover and simmer for 1 hour.

Lift lamb from sauce and transfer to a plate. Add olives, dates, parsley, cilantro, honey and sesame seeds to pan, crushing dates with the back of a spoon to thicken gravy. Simmer for 5 minutes. If sauce is too thick, add wine until sauce reaches desired consistency. If sauce is too thin, simmer until reduced to desired consistency. Return lamb to pan and heat through. Garnish servings with cilantro, olives and dates.

Servings: 6

INDEX